Discovering Science

From Cycle to Spaceship
The story of transport

Michael Pollard

Facts On File Publications
New York, New York ● Oxford, England

W9-ADY-015

Contents

NOTE TO THE READER: while you are reading this book you will notice that certain words appear in **bold type**. This is to indicate a word listed in the Glossary on page 45. This glossary gives brief explanations of words which may be new to you.

Acknowlegements

The Publishers wish to thank the following organizations for their invaluable assistance in the preparation of this book.

British Aerospace
Canadian Pacific
NASA

British Hovercraft
Cincinnatti Milicron
SNCF — French Railways

Photographic credits

t = top   b = bottom   l = left   r = right   c = center

5 ZEFA; 6 The Hutchison Library: 7t, 7b, 13 ZEFA; 14 British Aerospace; 16 Canadian Pacific; 17 SNCF — French Railways; 18, 22, 24, 24/25 25, 29 ZEFA; 30 Chris Fairclough; 31 British Hovercraft; 34 ZEFA; 38 Cincinnatti Milicron; 40, 42 NASA

Illustrations by Paul Doherty, Keith Duran/Linden Artists, Peter Endsleigh Castle, George Fryer/Linden Artists, Tony Gibbons/Linden Artists, Sallie Alane Reason, Brian Watson/Linden Artists

Discovering Science/From Cycle to Spaceship

Copyright © BLA Publishing Limited 1987

First published in the United States of America by Facts on File, Inc. 460 Park Avenue South, New York, New York 10016.

Library of Congress Catalog Card Number:
87-80098

Designed and produced by BLA Publishing Limited, East Grinstead, Sussex, England.

A member of the **Ling Kee Group**
LONDON · HONG KONG · TAIPEI · SINGAPORE · NEW YORK

Printed in Italy by New Interlitho

10 9 8 7 6 5 4 3 2 1

Moving around

We move around the world for many reasons. Some people go to work by car, bus or train. We travel to do our shopping. Sometimes we travel by plane or ship when we go on holiday. Our lives would be very different if we did not have **transport**.

Transport and energy

Today, wherever you go, you see wheels. Can you imagine what life would be like without them? There would be no bicycles, no cars and no trains. Without wheels you would have no means of transport on land. You would only be able to move around on foot.

The first people on Earth lived two million years ago. They were on the move all the time. They had no **machines** to help them.

The wheel was one of the first machines to be invented. People lived without wheels for a very long time. They began to use wheels only 5000 years ago.

At that time, carts with wheels were pulled by oxen. This helped people to travel further and to move heavy loads. All the oxen needed was grass to eat and water to drink. This gave these animals the **energy** to do heavy work for their owners.

Living and moving

▲ Cars and trucks cannot be used in the mountain tracks of Tibet. Pack animals are used instead.

Humans and all other animals are like machines. They can move about and do work. Some machines, like cars, need **fuel** to produce energy. So do animals. Their fuel is food and water.

Our bodies change the food we eat into energy. Energy gives us the power to move and to work. We can walk, run, swim, lift things and carry them. The more work we do, the more food we need. Some animals can move faster than humans. Others are slower, but they can carry heavier loads. In many parts of the world, people still use animals to help them with their work.

Moving in mountains

Tibet, in Central Asia, is a land of very high mountains. There are few roads wide enough for traffic on wheels. The Tibetans use animals called yaks to carry their loads. These animals are long-haired. They move slowly but surely on the narrow tracks.

Moving and working in mountains is difficult. The air is thinner and it is harder to breathe. The people who live all the time in mountains have **adapted** to life in thin air. They have larger lungs, so they can breathe in more air.

Moving in deserts

In the sandy deserts of Africa, camels are often used to carry loads. They have large feet which do not sink into the sand. They can go without food and water for days. Camels have adapted to moving and working in hot deserts.

The Eskimos of Northern Canada live in a different kind of desert. It is an icy waste land called the tundra. The Eskimos use husky dogs to pull their sledges. The thick coats of the huskies keep out the cold.

Walking and running

How fast can you run? A fit athlete can run a short distance at about 32 kph (20 mph). People who run in marathon races move at about 12 kph (7.5 mph). This is about twice the speed of normal walking.

The fastest land animal is the cheetah, which lives in Africa. It can run at over 80 kph (50 mph), but only for a short distance. Greyhounds can run at about 56 kph (35 mph). A tortoise is very slow indeed. It would take several days to travel one kilometer. But a tortoise has to carry its home on its back!

> I carry my house with me. When I want to rest, I tuck in my head and my feet.

Wheels

How would you move a heavy load if there were no wheels to help you? You could drag it along the ground. You might need other people to help you. It would be hard work.

Another idea would be to use rollers. This would be slow. You would have to keep stopping to move the rollers to the front. The idea of wheels may have come from the use of tree-trunks as rollers. The first wheels may just have been slices of tree-trunk. They were fixed to the sides of a cart.

Wheels and axles

The next step was to fit two wheels to an **axle**. The axle was fixed under the cart and the wheels turned around the centre, or hub, of the axle. The wheels rubbed against the axle, and they soon wore down. The axle hole became too large. The wheels became loose and soon fell off.

▲ The first wheels were made by cutting slices from tree trunks. This wheel dates from 3000 BC.

You will see why we do not have this problem now if you think of a bicycle wheel. Inside the hub there is a set of ball-bearings. These are hard metal balls that roll as the wheel turns. They roll easily because they are **lubricated** with oil.

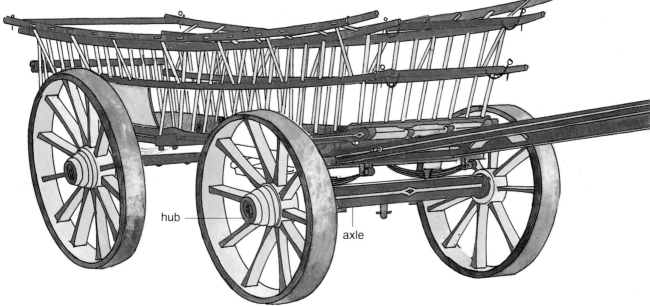

hub

axle

Remember to lubricate your skates with oil now and again. This will make the skates run smoothly.

shape slightly when they go over bumps in the road. This smooths out the bumps so that people do not feel them.

Pneumatic tires must be filled to just the right **pressure**. If they are too soft, it will be difficult to steer. If they are pumped up too hard, the tires will not smooth out the bumps.

Fun on eight wheels

Do you own a pair of roller-skates? If you do, you move along on ball-bearings when you use them. Each of the four wheels on each skate moves on ball-bearings. The smallest push of your foot makes the wheels go round easily.

Pneumatic tires

If solid wheels were fitted to cars and trucks, they would give a hard and bumpy ride. Road wheels have **pneumatic** tires. These are pumped up with air. They are soft enough to change

The bicycle

There are many kinds of machine that help us move around. Most of them have **engines** to give power. The bicycle is a machine that does not need an engine. It uses human energy instead. It changes your energy into movement. Bicycles do not need fuel, so they are quiet, and cheap to run.

A bicycle changes the up-and-down movement of your feet to the round-and-round movement of the wheels. Very little effort is wasted when you ride a bicycle. It takes less effort to cover a distance than if you were running. You can also go faster.

In some countries, bicycles are the main type of transport. They are cheap to use and last for a long time. People use them to go to work or to the shops.

Pedal power

The **pedals** on a bicycle are fixed to a wheel with teeth on it. This is called the **chainwheel**. A chain passes around this wheel and fits on to the teeth. The chain is connected to the back wheel. Here, it

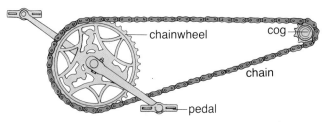

chainwheel · cog · chain · pedal

is passed around another toothed wheel called the cog. When your feet move the pedals around, the chain carries the energy of your body to the cog. When the cog turns, the back wheel turns with it.

How do gears work?

The chainwheel and the cog are **gears** that are linked by the chain. There are more teeth on the chainwheel than there are on the cog. So the cog goes around

several times for each turn of the chainwheel. If you make one turn of the pedals, your feet move about as far as in one walking pace. The bicycle travels about three times as far. It does more work for the same amount of effort.

Some bicycles are fitted with several gears. Each gear changes the number of times the back wheel turns for each turn of the pedals. The gears with few teeth are the high gears. They turn the back wheel faster for each turn of the pedals. You have to change to a lower gear to help you up a hill.

What difference can you see between the gears on the bicycle on the left and those in the drawing below?

Take two coins and put them down flat next to each other so that they touch. Now turn one coin against the other. You will see that they turn in opposite directions.

▼ A bicycle chain has an important job to do. Without a chain, as in the left hand picture, the chainwheel and cog would turn in opposite directions. Then you would need to pedal backwards to go forwards!

These two toothed wheels are connected by a chain. They turn in the same direction.

Two toothed wheels turn in opposite directions when not connected by a chain.

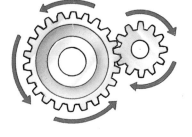

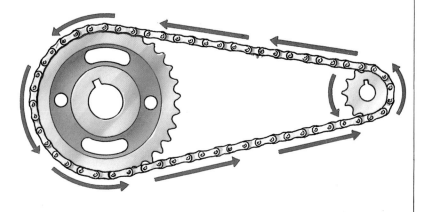

Forces at work

Perhaps you keep your bicycle in a shed. It may stay there for days on end without moving. Nothing will move unless a **force** is used to make it do so. When you do take it out, you use your own force to make the bicycle move. The harder you push on the pedals, the faster the bicycle will go.

When you come to a downhill slope, the bicycle free-wheels. On a long hill it goes on moving. When you want to stop it, you have to use the force of your hands to put the brakes on.

We make use of forces all the time. When two people use a hand saw to saw wood they can work together. They push and pull the saw backwards and forwards to cut through the wood. There are also natural forces that we use. Riding a bicycle with the wind behind you is easy. The force of the wind helps to push you along.

How gravity works

There is a natural force called **gravity**. It affects us all the time. Gravity pulls everything towards the Earth. If we drop something, it falls to the ground because of gravity. If there were no gravity you would not be able to stand. You would float off into space.

The force of gravity makes it easier to go downhill than to climb uphill. If you go on a rollercoaster ride at an amusement park, you feel the force of gravity. It sends you plunging downhill. Then your speed carries you up over the next climb.

What is friction?

Another natural force is called **friction**. This is the slowing-down that happens when two surfaces rub against each other. When friction takes place, some of the energy is turned into heat. Have you ever rubbed your hands together in cold weather? It is friction that warms them.

Friction can be used to slow down movement or to stop it. Car brakes work by using the friction between the brake pads and the brake disc. Car tires have patterns called **treads** cut into them. These make the surface of the tire rough. There is friction where the tread meets the rough surface of the road. This helps to grip the road if it is wet or icy.

Making things work well

There are many different types of transport. There are cars, buses, trains, ships and planes. They all need fuel to make their engines work. The engines burn the fuel to make energy for movement.

Fuel costs a lot of money so it is important not to waste it. We want machines to work well. We also want them to use as little fuel as possible. Then they are **efficient** machines.

There are some forces that make machines less efficient. One of these forces is gravity. Gravity makes it hard for planes to take off. An airliner has to use a lot of fuel to climb up into the sky from the runway. The plane meets the **resistance** of air as it gathers speed. This is called **drag**. All moving things are slowed down by drag.

Streamlining

Air resists and slows down any object that moves through it. Most kinds of transport can be made to work better by cutting down this resistance. A car or a plane shaped like a box with square sides would not be efficient. There would be too much drag. This is why cars and planes are streamlined. Their bodies are shaped and curved smoothly. This makes air flow around them more easily.

Water slows down moving things in the same way that air does. Ships have pointed fronts and curved sides. These help ships to cut through the water.

▼ A plane is tested for drag in a wind tunnel. Smoke is forced over the model at very high speed. Scientists can then see if the plane will move efficiently through air.

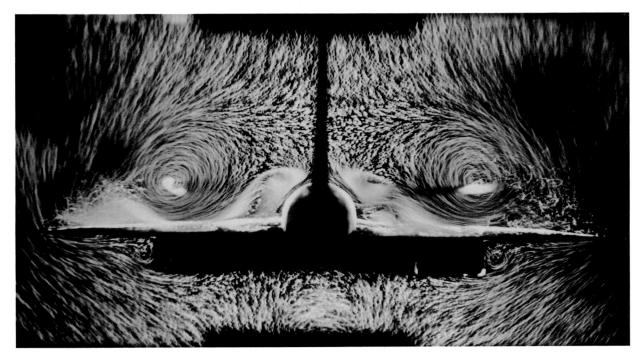

Keep your hand flat and push it through water. You can feel the resistance as quite a strong force, slowing your hand down. Now curve your hand and pass it through the water. You will find that it moves more easily. Can you see why ships have pointed fronts and curved sides?

Why oil?

All machines have to be cared for. The moving parts must run smoothly. If you own a bicycle, stand it upside down, as in the picture. Now turn the pedals slowly. You will be able to see where the moving parts rub against each other.

These are the parts which you should oil often. Oil will help the chain, the pedals and the wheels to run smoothly. All machines and engines have to be oiled. This reduces friction and makes them work well.

▼ Oil helps a bicycle to work well.

High-speed trains

Railways are an efficient means of transport. They can carry many more people than buses can. They can also travel faster.

Railways work well for many reasons. There are no steep hills on a railway. The track is smooth and straight, and there are no sharp bends. A heavy train can keep up a high speed over a long distance. Each train has a large part of the track to itself. Signals are used to make sure that there is a large gap between one train and the next one. This makes railway travel very safe.

Trains build up speed slowly because they are very heavy. Once a train has reached a fast speed, its weight helps to keep it rolling. The faster a train is going, and the heavier it is, the longer it takes for a train to slow down. The driver has to start slowing down a long time before he reaches a station. He has to think of two things, the weight of the train, and its speed.

The hard steel wheels of a train may run on a smooth steel track. There is little friction, so little energy is wasted.

The wheels of a car or truck have rubber tires. Road surfaces are often rough and bumpy. A lot of energy is wasted, because of friction.

High-speed trains

In some countries, high-speed trains run between large cities. In Britain, they are called '125s'. They reach a speed of 200 kph (125 mph). In France, high-speed trains are called 'TGVs'. They travel even faster. The Japanese high-speed trains are called 'Bullet Trains'. Many of the old railway tracks had to be rebuilt for high-speed trains. The track had to be as straight as possible. All the bends in the old track had to be smoothed out. Then the trains could run at a fast speed without having to slow down.

Going round corners

A curve in a railway track is like a part of a circle. A train is pulled towards the centre as it travels around the curve. This force, and the curved track, helps the train to change direction.

The force does not work if the train is going too fast. The weight and speed of the train will force it to carry on in a

▲ This picture shows a French TGV traveling at high speed.

straight line. It cannot change direction and the train will come off the rails.

When you cycle around a bend, you lean inwards to make it easier. Trains cannot do this, so the track is given a slope, called a **camber**. The rail on the outside is higher than the rail on the inside. This keeps the train safely on the track.

Flying through the air

Most birds and insects are made for flying. Insects move their wings so fast that it is hard to see how they work. If you watch birds flying, you can see more easily how they do it. They flap their wings up and down to take off and to keep flying. They spread their wings to glide on currents of air. When they dive, they fold their wings close to their bodies.

Some birds can keep flying over long distances, by making use of the wind. Birds are streamlined just like planes are.

Human flight

Have you ever thought that it would be fun to fly like a bird? We would all like to

do this, and so overcome gravity. Some people have even tried to fly.

They strapped wings on to their arms and tried flapping them. No one has ever made this work, though many have tried. Wings would have to be very large to lift a human body into the air. The arms would not be strong enough to flap the wings.

Slowing down gravity

A **parachute** is a thing for slowing down the force of gravity. You can make a model parachute yourself. You will need

Can you describe how this bird is moving its wings?

Gliders

Gliders are planes without engines. They have narrow bodies and long thin wings. Gliders are made of light materials.

Gliders cannot take off on their own. They have to be towed along the ground, or through the air. Once in the air, the pilot uses warm air currents, called **thermals**, to give the glider **lift**. The glider is carried up by the thermals in a spiral pattern.

At the top of the spiral, the pilot glides downwards and looks for another thermal to give the plane lift. If there is no thermal to be found, the glider returns to Earth and lands.

some string, a piece of cloth about 30 cm (12 in) square, and a stone. Tie a string to each corner of the cloth. Put the stone in a paper bag and tie this to the loose ends of the strings. Roll your parachute into a ball and throw it high in the air. It will open out and float slowly back to Earth. When the cloth spreads out, it traps air underneath it. This slows the parachute down as it falls.

▼ Gliders use thermals to gain height.

Light aircraft

Light aircraft carry a pilot and two or three passengers only. All planes fly in the same way, whether they are big or small.

There are four forces at work when a plane flies. As a plane passes through the air, it meets resistance. This is called drag. Weight is due to the force of gravity. It pulls a plane towards the ground. A plane needs **thrust** to overcome drag, and lift to overcome weight.

The engine provides the thrust. If there is not enough thrust, a plane will **stall** and drop quickly. The wings give a plane lift. If there is not enough lift, the plane will not take off or stay in the air.

Propeller engines

Most light planes have **propeller** engines. Propellers are made of wood or light metal. They have two, three or four blades. Each blade is slightly twisted.

As the propeller turns, its blades twist into the air. They push air out behind them. In this way they pull the plane through the air. The propeller gives the plane thrust so that it can fly through the air.

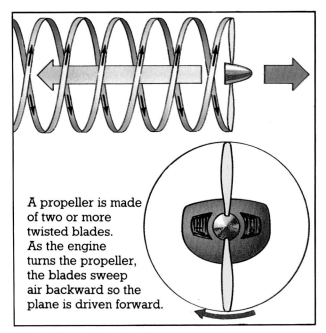

A propeller is made of two or more twisted blades. As the engine turns the propeller, the blades sweep air backward so the plane is driven forward.

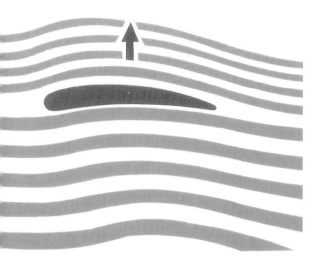

The wings

The wings of a plane are made in a special shape. It is called an **aerofoil**. The top surface of a wing is curved, but the bottom surface is almost flat. The whole wing is tilted slightly upwards so that it pushes against the air.

As a plane moves forward, the wing cuts through the air. The air pressure above the wing is lower than it is underneath. The higher pressure on the bottom surface gives the plane lift.

Controlling flight

A plane must be able to gain or lose height, and to steer left or right. There are moving parts to do this on the wings and tailplane. The pilot can control these from the cockpit. **Elevators** on the tail can be moved up or down to make a plane climb or dive. On the rear edge of each wing are **ailerons**. On the tail **fin** is a hinged **rudder**.

The ailerons and rudder are used to make turns. They make the plane tilt as it changes direction. This is called banking. The pilot must not bank too sharply or the plane will stall.

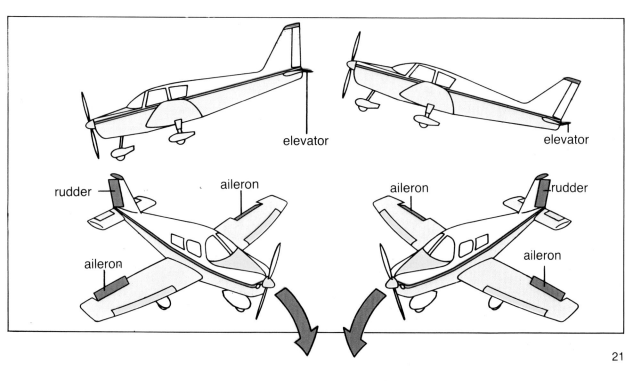

elevator

elevator

rudder

aileron

aileron

aileron

rudder

aileron

Jet aircraft

Light planes carry only a few people. Large airliners can carry as many as 500 people. They may be in the air for 12 hours or more. A long trip can cover thousands of miles.

Airliners need powerful engines to make these journeys. They have to fly a long way without stopping for more fuel. Propeller engines are still used on some planes, but jet engines are more efficient. Airliners have two, three or four jet engines.

Propeller engines pull a plane through the air. Jet engines work by pushing it. Hot gases pour out of the back of the engine. The gases give the thrust to make the plane move forward.

▼ You can see how large a jet engine is, compared with the man nearby.

What is a jet?

Blow up a balloon. Now let it go without tying the neck. The air rushes out in one direction. The balloon goes off in the other direction. This is called a **reaction**.

A jet engine works in much the same way. Hot gases are pushed out at the back of the engine. So the plane moves forward.

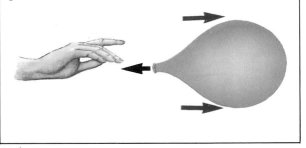

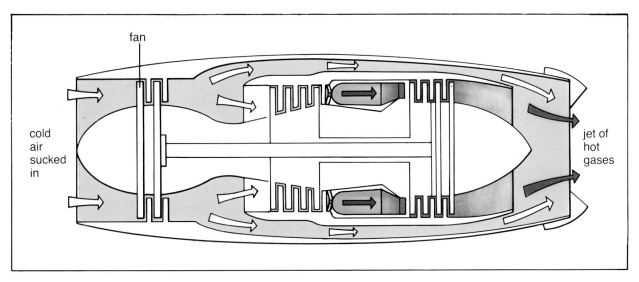

A jet engine

Most jet engines are turbofans. In the front of the engine is a fan with many blades on it. This spins and draws air into the engine. The air is packed tight, or **compressed**. It is mixed with burning fuel inside the engine.

This makes very hot gases which rush to escape from the engine. They stream out of the engine as a powerful jet. The plane is thrust forward. Some of the air is led around the engine without being heated. This helps to cool the engine.

Take-off and landing

When a heavy plane takes off it needs as much thrust and lift as possible. The plane has to gain height quickly. The engines are at full power, and the wings provide the lift.

The wing of an airliner is not made in one fixed piece. Parts of the wing can be moved by the pilot. There are flaps that can be moved out to make the wing larger. These are used to give the plane lift for taking off and climbing. As the plane gains height, the flaps are pulled back.

Spoilers are also fitted to the wings. These can be raised to help the airliner lose speed as it comes in to land.

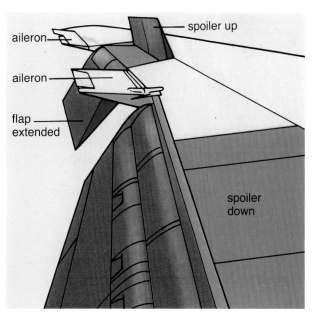

Airport

A large airport is like a town. Thousands of people work there. It has its own roads, shops, police and fire services. Planes take off and land day and night. The busiest airport in the world is at Chicago. More than 4.5 million passengers pass through this airport each year. Over 2000 planes land or take off every day of the year.

Passengers and freight

At a busy airport, planes take off and land every few minutes. The airport staff has to look after people from all parts of the world.

When passengers arrive at an airport, they go to the check-in desk. At the desk, a computer checks each person's ticket against the flight number. Each

▲ This is Gatwick airport, in the south of England. Passengers have a direct rail link to London.

passenger is given a seat number. The computer lists all the passengers for each flight. It also lists the baggage weight and the freight to be carried by the plane.

Air traffic control

Aircraft have to be controlled, just like road and rail traffic. At an airport, this is done from the control tower. Controllers are in charge of the movement of all planes on the runways and taxiways. They give their orders by radio.

Another group of controllers is in charge of planes coming in to land, and those which have just taken off. They have **radar** to help them.

▼ Each airline has one or more check-in desks. You show your ticket and have your baggage weighed.

The controllers use radar to watch the movement of planes. Each plane shows up as a 'blip' of light on a screen. The screen shows where all planes are in the sky around the airport.

Loading

Before a flight, each plane is checked by the ground staff. They have to make sure that the plane is ready for flight. Then the plane is loaded with the right amount of fuel for the flight.

Some planes carry freight as well as passengers. The freight is loaded so that the weight is spread evenly. Then the crew come on board. The captain checks that everything has been done correctly. Then the passengers start to come on board. The flight is ready to begin.

▼ On this Boeing 747 freighter the nose is raised so that freight can be loaded into the cargo hold.

Keeping afloat

Some things, like wood, float in water. Other things, such as stone, sink to the bottom. The first humans found that they could move on the water by sitting on logs. Then they hollowed out logs to make the first boats. These 'dugout' boats floated better because they were lighter than solid logs.

Boats do not have to be made of wood to float. They can be made of metal, even though metal is very heavy. A boat must be broad and hollow in shape in order to float well. It presses down on the water. As it does this, the boat pushes some of the water aside, and some downwards. This water pushes back on the boat and supports it. This is called **upthrust**.

If a load is put in a boat, the boat will sink deeper into the water. The boat pushes down harder on the water.

It will still float because the upthrust is greater. But if the load is too heavy, the boat will sink.

▼ In this cut-away drawing of a tanker you can see where the oil is stored. Do you think it is important for the oil to be spread evenly in the storage space?

The Plimsoll mark

If you watch a ship being loaded, you will be able to see the Plimsoll mark. You can see it down near the water line.

'This shows the safe level to which a ship may be loaded. There are different levels for fresh and for salt water. Fresh water is lighter than salt water. A ship floats deeper in fresh water than in salt water. The two marks **F** and **TF** are for fresh water and tropical fresh water. The marks on the right of the picture are for salt water. The letters **L** and **R** stand for Lloyds Register. This is the office in London which makes the safety rules.

Balancing the load

If a ship has too heavy a load, it may sink in rough seas. This is why there is a line on the Plimsoll mark, showing WNA. This shows the safe load level for **W**inter in the **N**orth **A**tlantic. There are rough seas there in the winter. There is another line for **T**ropical seas. The seas are calmer in the tropics. The other two salt water marks are for **S**ummer and **W**inter.

When a ship is loaded, the weight of the cargo must be spread evenly. Crates and containers must be roped down. Then they will not move if the ship meets rough seas.

Bulk cargoes like oil and grain cannot be roped. They are split up between a number of holds. This stops the whole cargo moving in rough seas. The ship shown in the picture is a very large oil tanker. The oil is carried in several holds.

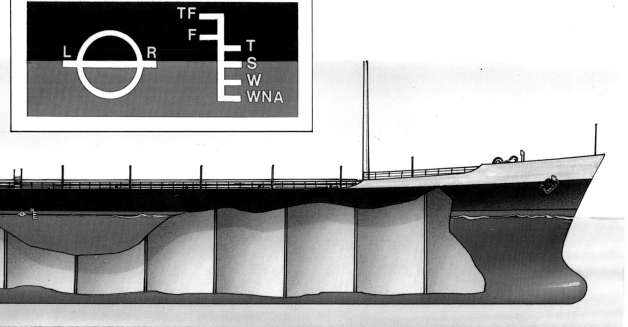

Across the oceans

Many of the ships that cross the oceans are very large. Because these ships are so large and heavy, they cannot change course quickly. It may take several miles for one of these ships to stop. Their crews have to keep a close watch for other ships near them.

Some oil tankers are more than 350 yards long. The largest of these can carry about 500,000 tons of oil. These vast ships move through the water at 16 mph.

Propellers and turbines

All ships are slowed down by drag as they move through the water. The propellers give thrust to overcome the drag. There are usually four or more blades on a ship's propeller. The huge propeller turns smoothly and quite slowly. It pushes, or thrusts, the water backwards. This pushes the ship forwards.

The power to drive some ships comes from steam **turbines**. Water is boiled to make steam. Jets of steam are piped

into the turbine. This is a shaft with a large number of blades set around it. The force of the steam makes the blades and shaft turn. Power from the spinning shaft reaches the propellers through a set of gears.

Rough seas

Ships often meet bad weather. Then the seas are rough and there are large waves. When a ship meets waves head-on, it causes pitching. This is an up-and-down movement from bow to stern.

Waves from the side cause a side-to-side movement called rolling. These are the movements that make people feel seasick.

Modern ships are fitted with **stabilizers**. These are fins on each side of a ship. They can be pushed out into the water. They help to stop the ship from rolling in rough seas. When they are not needed they are drawn back.

Container ships

The old way of loading ships was to fill the holds with crates and boxes of different shapes and sizes. The new way is to use containers.

Containers are large metal boxes, all of the same size and shape. They fit neatly in a ship's hold or on its decks. At ports they are easily loaded or unloaded by cranes.

The containers can be taken to or from the port by road or rail. They fit neatly on to lorries or railway trucks. Each truck carries one large container.

▼ A container ship being loaded. Do you see why it is important for all the containers to be the same size?

Skimming the waves

Ships move very slowly. Few can move faster than 45 kph (28 mph), and most ships are far slower. This is because there is so much drag from the water.

Boats that skim the top of the waves instead of pushing through them can travel much faster. There are two types of boat that skim the waves. They are the **hydrofoil** and the **hovercraft**. Both types of boat can travel at speeds of more than 80 kph (50 mph).

The hydrofoil

When it is still, a hydrofoil looks like a normal boat. As it starts to move, it rises up from the water. It looks as if it is on legs or stilts. There are **foils** on the ends of the stilts, just under the water. These are shaped like the wings of a plane. The top surface of a foil is curved. The bottom surface is flat.

When the boat is moving, high pressure underneath the foil lifts the boat above the water. The propeller stays in the water and drives the boat forward. The slope of the foils can be altered. They can raise the boat higher or let it lie lower in the water.

▲ A hydrofoil looks like a boat on stilts. The hull hardly touches the water when the boat is at full speed.
▼

The hovercraft

The hovercraft moves on a cushion of air. Large fans inside the craft pump air down towards the water. The cushion of air forces the craft to rise above the water. A 'skirt' around the bottom of the craft stops the air from escaping.

The fans are driven by gas turbines. These also drive the craft's propellers. The propellers are fixed on masts above the deck. They can be turned to help with steering.

Hovercraft can be used over land as well as over water. They can move from one to the other without changing speed. They do not need to unload at a port. Hovercraft can be used over fields or swamps. They cannot be used on uneven or hilly ground.

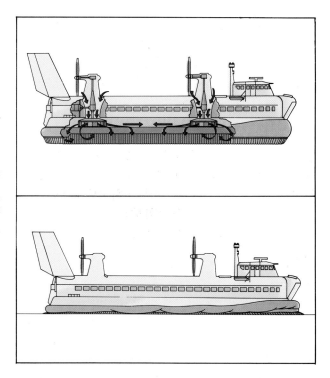

Hydrofoils and hovercraft cannot be used in rough seas. They are used mainly on lakes, rivers and for short sea crossings. The largest hydrofoil is 65 m (213 ft) long. It moves at a speed of 92 kph (58 mph). The largest hovercraft can travel at 120 kph (75 mph).

▲ A hovercraft can leave the water and move up on to the land at the end of a journey.
▼

The car engine

A bicycle turns the up-and-down movement of your feet on the pedals into the round-and-round movement of the wheels. A car engine works in a similar way. The **pistons** move up and down. They drive the **crankshaft**. The crankshaft goes round and round. It drives the wheels.

Pistons are made of metal. They fit tightly into steel **cylinders**. There is just enough room for the pistons to move up and down. Rods connect the pistons with the crankshaft.

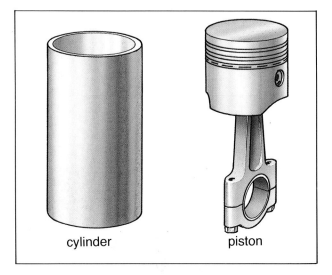

cylinder   piston

What is internal combustion?

Cars have internal **combustion** engines. Combustion is burning. You cannot see combustion in a car engine because it takes place inside the cylinders. The burning gives out smoke and fumes which come out of the **exhaust** pipe.

In a car engine, fuel is mixed with air. The mixture is burnt by an electric spark. The burning gases **expand** and take up more space. There is only one way for them to escape. They push the piston down the cylinder to get out.

The piston rods make the crankshaft turn. When the engine is running, thousands of piston movements take place in one minute. Each one keeps the crankshaft turning. The movement of the crankshaft turns the road wheels.

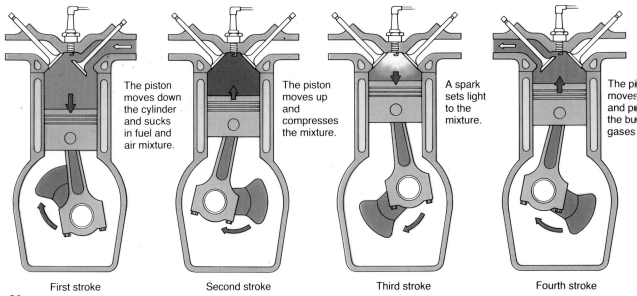

The piston moves down the cylinder and sucks in fuel and air mixture.

The piston moves up and compresses the mixture.

A spark sets light to the mixture.

The p moves and p the bu gases

First stroke   Second stroke   Third stroke   Fourth stroke

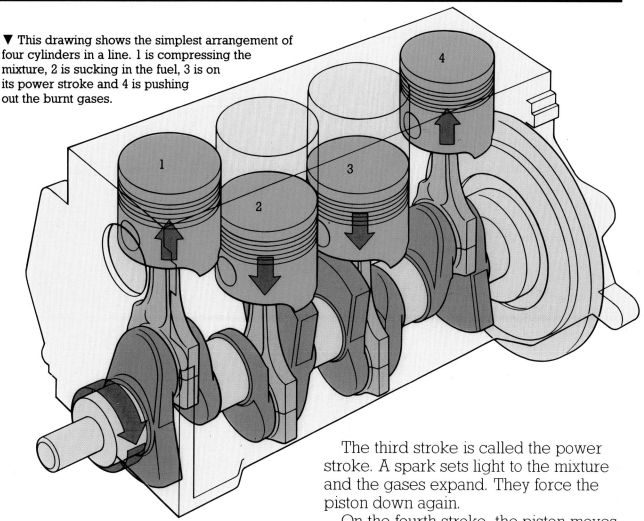

▼ This drawing shows the simplest arrangement of four cylinders in a line. 1 is compressing the mixture, 2 is sucking in the fuel, 3 is on its power stroke and 4 is pushing out the burnt gases.

The four-stroke idea

Most cars have four-**stroke** engines. There are four movements in a cylinder from one firing to the next.

On the first stroke, the piston moves down the cylinder. It sucks in the fuel and air mixture through a **valve**. Valves open and close.

On the second stroke, the piston moves up again. As it does so it packs the mixture tight, or compresses it.

The third stroke is called the power stroke. A spark sets light to the mixture and the gases expand. They force the piston down again.

On the fourth stroke, the piston moves up. It pushes the burnt gases out through the exhaust valve. The piston is now ready to start the whole process again.

The four-cylinder engine

All this movement takes place inside one cylinder. An engine with one cylinder produces a jerky movement. Car engines have at least four cylinders. Some have as many as twelve. The cylinders fire one after another. The more there are, the smoother the engine runs.

The power system

The power of a car's engine has to be passed to the road wheels. The **system** that does this is called the **transmission**. In some cars, the power goes to the rear wheels. These are the driving wheels. Many cars have front-wheel drive. Cars and trucks used for moving over rough country have four-wheel drive. Each wheel is a driving wheel.

The drive system

In a car with rear-wheel drive, the power from the engine has to pass to the rear wheels. The engine's crankshaft turns a flywheel. The flywheel passes on the power to the drive shaft. On the way, the power passes through the **clutch** and the **gearbox**.

The gears change the amount of power that the driver needs. Low or bottom gear gives high power for starting, or for going up hills. The driver uses top gear when less power is needed. This may be for keeping a steady speed on a level road.

The clutch disconnects the power between the flywheel and the gearbox. It allows the driver to change gear. The driver can use the clutch pedal and gear lever to disconnect power and choose another gear.

▼ This is where you find the transmission system in a car.

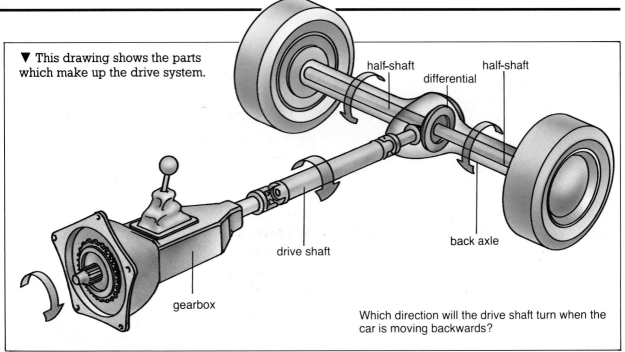

▼ This drawing shows the parts which make up the drive system.

half-shaft

differential

half-shaft

drive shaft

back axle

gearbox

Which direction will the drive shaft turn when the car is moving backwards?

Differential

On rear-wheel drive cars, the drive shaft runs from the front of the car to the back. Power from the shaft has to change direction to drive the road wheels. Each road wheel is turned by a half-shaft.

Each half-shaft is connected to the differential. They can turn at different speeds. This lets the wheels move at different speeds on a corner. The outside wheel has to travel further than the inside wheel.

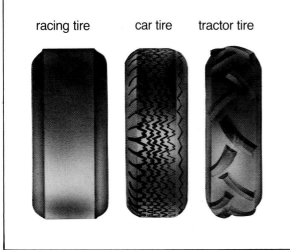

racing tire   car tire   tractor tire

Road wheels

Only a small part of each car tire touches the road at any one time. All the power of the engine passes through the small patches on to the road. Each tire has a deep **tread**, so that it can grip the road. When the tread wears down a tire becomes smooth. Then it does not grip the road so well, and the car might skid on a wet or icy road.

All systems go!

You are able to keep a healthy body if all its parts work well. It is the same with a car. A car is made up of a number of parts, or systems. They all work together, and must be kept in good working order.

Brakes

Brakes slow down a car or stop it. Most cars have disc brakes at the front, and drum brakes at the rear. A disc or drum goes round with the wheel. When the driver brakes, brake pads, or shoes, press against the disc or drum. The wheel is slowed by friction.

▶ This diagram shows where the different systems in a car are found.

The fuel system

The fuel system feeds the engine with a mixture of fuel and air. A pump brings the fuel from the tank to a part of the engine called the **carburetor**. Here the fuel is mixed with air to make a **vapor**. Then the vapor is drawn into each cylinder, where it is fired by a spark.

The electrical system

Cars cannot work without electricity. A **battery** gives power to start the engine. Once the engine is running, some of its power is used to make electricity. This produces sparks in each cylinder. Some electricity goes to the battery to charge it. The rest can be used to make the lights, wipers and other parts work.

Exhaust

The exhaust system takes away the burnt gases from the cylinders. They pass along a pipe which goes beneath the car. They go through the **muffler**. This cuts down the noise. Finally, the gases pass out into the air from the tail pipe.

Cooling

Engines are damaged if they are not kept cool. In most cars, water is used in the cooling system. It is pumped through pipes around the engine. The water carries the heat away to the radiator. A fan draws in cold air from in front of the car. The air cools the water.

Steering

The steering system connects the steering wheel with the front road wheels. Moving the wheel turns the steering column. A set of gears connects the column with the tie rod. When the tie rod moves, it points the front wheels in a new direction.

Suspension

The **suspension** system smooths out bumps and shocks from the road. It helps give you a nice, smooth ride. Springs fitted between each wheel and the body frame **absorb** any shocks or bumps. The springs are stopped from bouncing back too much. Each wheel has its own set of springs.

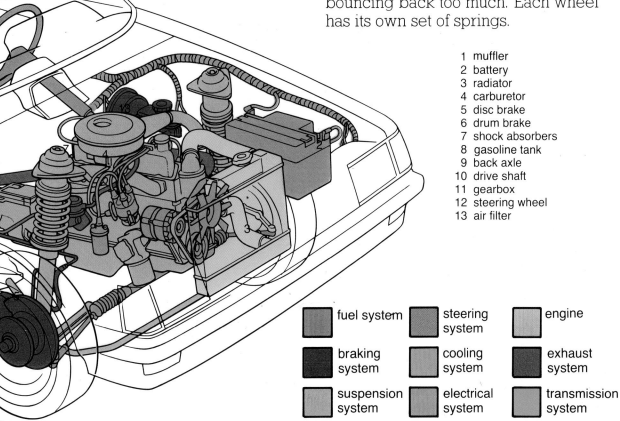

1 muffler
2 battery
3 radiator
4 carburetor
5 disc brake
6 drum brake
7 shock absorbers
8 gasoline tank
9 back axle
10 drive shaft
11 gearbox
12 steering wheel
13 air filter

fuel system

braking system

suspension system

steering system

cooling system

electrical system

engine

exhaust system

transmission system

Production line

Millions of new cars are made in the world's factories each year. They are put together from thousands of different parts.

Only the most expensive cars are made one at a time. Most cars are made on a production line. Each worker does one job on each car as it moves slowly past. The car moves on to the next worker who does the next job. This kind of work is called mass production.

The body shell

The sides, roof, back and floor of a car make up the body shell. This is made of pressed steel. Each body panel is stamped out of a steel sheet and pressed into shape. The panels are joined together to make up the body shell. Then it is ready to move on to the main **assembly** line. Here all the other parts are added.

Using robots

A **weld** is a way of joining sheets of steel by melting them in one spot. When they cool and harden they are fixed tight together. In a car body shell, there may be as many as 10,000 welds.

Body shells are welded by robots. A robot is a machine that can be 'told' to do the same job time and time again. It takes its 'orders' from a computer. Robots are faster and more accurate than human workers. They do not make mistakes and they do not get tired.

Four stages in the assembly of a car. After the
body shell is painted, it is lowered on to the
main assembly line.

The assembly line

In a car factory there is a main assembly
line. There are also a number of smaller
ones. Each of these puts together a
different part of the car. One assembles
the engine, another the body shell,
another the drive system, and so on.
Each then feeds its bit to the main line.
This has to be done in the right order.

The engine, drive shaft and wheel
hubs reach the main line first. The body
shell is lowered on to them. As the car
moves along the line, more parts are
fixed to it. Some of the workers stand at
the side of the line. Others work in pits
beneath it. Each piece of work is
planned so that there are no hold-ups.

When a finished car comes off the
line, it goes on to a set of rollers. The
engine is started up and all the systems
are checked. If all is well, the new car is
driven off to be stored.

The Shuttle

The future of space travel may now depend upon the Shuttle or some spaceship like it. In 1986, one of these blew up seconds after lift-off, killing all the crew. The United States then decided to stop all flights until they could be sure that this would never happen again.

The Shuttle looks like a large plane with rocket engines at the tail. It can carry a heavy load into space, and from space back to Earth again. The Shuttle is designed so that it can be used over and over again.

For the launch, it is attached to a large fuel tank and two booster rockets to give extra thrust. Two minutes after launch, the boosters are released. They float back to Earth by parachute and can be used again. Later, the large tank is dropped into the sea.

In orbit

The two engines of the Shuttle take over at a height of about 120 km (75 miles) above the Earth. They give the craft its final push. Then the Shuttle goes into **orbit** at a height of about 280 km (174 miles) above the Earth. No more power is needed while it orbits around the Earth.

The Shuttle has a cargo hold. It can take satellites into space and leave them there. There is room to store supplies for the crew. They can stay in space for up to one month.

external tank jettisoned

solid booster recovery

Landing the Shuttle

When the work is finished, the Shuttle returns to Earth. It has to slow down to come out of orbit. It does this by turning tail first and firing the engines.

The Shuttle turns nose first to enter the atmosphere. The heat shield glows red-hot with friction as it meets the resistance of air. From now on, no power is used to land. The Shuttle glides down to Earth. It lands like a normal plane on a very long runway.

Space stations

One day, spacecraft like the Shuttle may be used to build a large space station. Hundreds of flights would be needed to do this. Once built, the space station would have many uses. It could be used as a base for flights to the Moon, and to the planets.

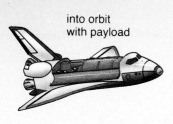

into orbit
with payload

re-entry: heat
shield glowing
red-hot with friction

gliding in
to land

Beyond the Earth

For hundreds of years people have wondered what it would be like to travel in space. Now we have begun to find out. The journeys into space that have been made so far are only the start.

Leaving the Earth

A spacecraft has to be launched by rocket to leave the Earth. It has to reach a speed of 40,000 kph (25,000 mph) to escape from the Earth's gravity. A tremendous thrust is needed to reach this speed, and to carry a load.

Rocket engines produce this thrust by burning gases. These pour out of the tail of the rocket. Rockets burn liquid **oxygen** and **hydrogen** as fuel.

A rocket, with its spacecraft, reaches space in a few minutes after blast-off. Then the spacecraft separates from the rocket, and goes on moving at the same speed. It can change direction by using small thrusters. There is no drag or gravity to slow down movement in space.

▼ This astronaut is using small rockets in his backpack to move through space.

▲ This craft carried the first two astronauts to their landing site on the Moon on 20th July 1969.

In 1969, two US **astronauts** landed on the Moon. They picked up pieces of moon rock and brought them back to Earth. The Moon is over 350,000 km (217,000 miles) from the Earth. No one had travelled so far into space before.

Moving in space

We do not often feel our weight on Earth. We are used to it. We sometimes notice it when a car starts quickly, or when the driver puts the brakes on hard. Then we feel forces called gravity forces, or G-forces for short. On Earth, we are used to a force of 1G.

At lift-off, an astronaut feels very heavy. He feels a force of 7G. When a spacecraft returns to Earth, it slows down very quickly as it enters the Earth's atmosphere. Astronauts may feel a force of 11G at this time.

There are no G-forces at all in space, because there is no gravity. People and objects float around inside the spacecraft. The astronauts must learn how to deal with these problems.

This artist's impression shows a spacecraft of the future approaching one of Saturn's moons.

Visiting the planets

People might one day try to visit one of the planets, but this will not be easy. Venus is the closest planet to Earth, but it is still 38 million km (23.5 million miles) away. Even if astronauts could travel this distance, there are other problems. The surface of Venus is so hot that it would melt metal. Mars is further away, but the surface is less uncomfortable.

Travel in the future

By the time that the first space station has been built there will be many more people on Earth. There may be 1000 million people more than there are in the world today. Most of these extra people will live and work in cities.

New, smaller cities will have to be built to take all these people. In the city of the future, traffic will be kept apart from people on foot. Ground level will be for shoppers and walkers only. Above this, there may be moving walkways. These will be for those who want to walk from one part of the city to another.

People driving to the city will park their cars at the edge. Then they will use public transport. Road and rail traffic coming to the city may move on enclosed tracks above the ground. In some cities of the world, these things are already being planned. In the future, moving around may be much easier than it is today.

Glossary

absorb: to take in or soak up

adapt: to change so as to suit changing surroundings and conditions

aerofoil: a surface, such as an aircraft wing, which is shaped to give lift when air flows over and under it

aileron: a hinged flap on the rear edge of an aircraft wing. It controls the rolling and banking movements of the aircraft

assembly: putting together the parts of something in a factory

astronaut: a person trained to fly in a spacecraft and work in space

axle: a shaft or rod around which one or more wheels turn

battery: a set of two or more electric cells which make and store electricity

camber: a tilt in the surface of something such as a road or railway track

carburetor: a part of a car engine which mixes air with gasoline to make a gas which powers a car's engine

chainwheel: a toothed wheel which carries a chain. On a bicycle, the pedals turn the chainwheel

clutch: the part of a car or other vehicle which connects the engine to the gearbox

combustion: burning. Internal combustion takes place inside the cylinders of an engine

compress: to squeeze together. A gas can be compressed

crankshaft: the main driving rod in an engine. It is connected to the pistons

cylinder: a hollow tube with circular walls. A part of an engine in which a piston moves up and down

drag: the force which slows a plane as it moves through the air, or a ship as it moves through water

efficient: working well

elevator: a hinged surface at the tail of an aircraft. It is moved up or down to make the aircraft climb or descend

energy: the power to do work

engine: a machine that uses fuel to do work

exhaust: the waste gases given off by an engine

expand: to become larger and take up more space

fin: a fixed blade on an aircraft which keeps it steady in flight; a tail fin

foil: a thin plate of metal

force: energy, power or strength. A force cannot be seen

friction: the force that slows down movement and produces heat when two surfaces are rubbed together

fuel: a material, such as oil or coal, that is used to make heat or power by burning

gear: a cog, or set of cogs, which transfer movement from one part of a machine to another part

gearbox: the container that holds the gears

gravity: a force we cannot see. Gravity gives people and objects weight

hovercraft: a vehicle that moves over land and water. It is held up by a cushion of air

hydrofoil: a boat that can skim the surface of the water on thin plates of metal called foils or hydrofoils

hydrogen: a gas that is lighter than air. It is the lightest gas and burns easily

lift: the force that keeps an aircraft in flight, helped by the shape of the wings

lubricate: to put oil or grease on the moving parts of a machine so that they will move freely

machine: something that uses energy or effort to do work. It helps us to do work more easily

muffler: part of the exhaust system of an engine. It cuts down the noise made by the escaping gases

orbit: the path of a satellite as it moves around another object in space

oxygen: a gas that is a part of air and water. Oxygen helps things to burn

parachute: an umbrella-shaped device used to slow down the speed at which a person or object falls

pedal: a lever pressed by the foot to make a bicycle move forward

piston: part of an engine that fits tightly in a cylinder and moves up and down inside it

pneumatic: worked by air or gas pressure

pressure: a pushing or squeezing force

propeller: a screw made of two or more blades used to drive a ship or plane forward

radar: radar is short for **ra**dio **d**etecting **a**nd **r**anging. Radio waves are bounced off an object. The return is timed to work out how far away the object is

reaction: an action or change in an opposite or different direction

resistance: something that acts against a force to slow down movement

rudder: the hinged surface, fixed to the tail end of a ship or aircraft, used for steering

spoiler: a flap on the wings of an aircraft that can be raised to slow it down

stabilizer: a device that helps to steady a ship and stop it rolling when it is moving through rough seas

stall: to lose flying speed and drop suddenly. A plane stalls when there is not enough lift to keep it flying

stroke: one movement in a set of movements

suspension: all the parts that support the body of a vehicle and help to smooth out the bumps

system: a set or group of things that work together

thermal: warm air rising above the ground. Thermals are used by glider pilots to help them gain height

thrust: a force which causes forward movement

transmission: the system in a car that carries power from the engine to the wheels

transport: carrying goods or people from one place to another

tread: the pattern cut into tires to help them grip the road

turbine: a shaft to which a number of curved blades are fixed. The turbine is made to turn at high speed by a gas or water

upthrust: an upward push or force that supports a floating object

valve: a device that allows fluids or gases to flow in one direction. The valves in a car engine open and close when the engine is working

vapor: a liquid in the form of a gas. A car engine burns gasoline vapor mixed with air

weld: to join two metals together by using heat or electricity